WORKBOOK
FOR

THE GRAPHIC NOVEL

NATIONAL GEOGRAPHIC LEARNING | **CENGAGE Learning**

Australia • Brazil • Japan • Korea • Mexico • Singapore • Spain • United Kingdom • United States

Workbook for Wuthering Heights: The Graphic Novel Emily Brontë

Publisher: Sherrise Roehr

Editor in Chief, Classical Comics: Clive Bryant

Development Editors: Brenden Layte, Cécile Engeln

Director of Product Marketing: Ellen Lees

Product Marketing Manager: Anders Bylund

Director of Content Production:
   Michael Burggren

Associate Content Project Manager:
   Mark Rzeszutek

Print Buyer: Mary Beth Hennebury

Compositor: MPS Limited

Cover Design: Gina Petti

Artwork: John M. Burns

Lettering: Jim Campbell

Design & Layout: Carl Andrews

For permission to use material from this text or product, submit all requests online at **www.cengage.com/permissions**
Further permissions questions can be emailed to
permissionrequest@cengage.com

ISBN: 978-1-111-83886-7

National Geographic Learning
20 Channel Center Street
Boston, MA 02210
USA

Cengage Learning is a leading provider of customized learning solutions with office locations around the globe, including Singapore, the United Kingdom, Australia, Mexico, Brazil and Japan.

Cengage Learning products are represented in Canada by Nelson Education, Ltd.

Visit Heinle online at **ngl.cengage.com**
Visit our corporate website at **www.cengage.com**

Printed in the United States of America
Print Number: 02   Print Year: 2020

CONTENTS

Before You Read

Worksheet 1 – Meet Emily Brontë

A. Choose the best answer to each question. Guess if you don't know the answer.

1. Emily Brontë was born in _____.
   a. England   **b.** Scotland   **c.** the United States   **d.** Ireland
2. Emily's sisters, _____, were also writers.
   a. Maria and Elizabeth   **b.** Anne and Charlotte   **c.** Charlotte and Elizabeth   **d.** Maria and Anne
3. Emily's father worked at a _____.
   a. factory   **b.** school   **c.** church   **d.** theater
4. Emily worked briefly as a _____ before she became a writer.
   a. teacher   **b.** governess   **c.** nurse   **d.** servant
5. Emily and Charlotte went to _____ to study languages.
   a. France   **b.** Belgium   **c.** Germany   **d.** Italy
6. Emily, her brother, and all her sisters died of _____.
   a. cancer   **b.** influenza   **c.** typhus   **d.** tuberculosis

Now read about Brontë on pp. 157–158 of *Wuthering Heights: The Graphic Novel* and find out if you were right.

B. Complete the timeline of Brontë's life.

Date	What Happened?
1818	Emily Brontë was born on July 30.
1821	
1838	
1846	
1847	
1848	
1849	
1850	
1855	

C. Emily Brontë published *Wuthering Heights* under the name Ellis Bell. Her sisters also used fake names. Why didn't they use their real names?

_____

_____

_____

Name: _____

Before You Read
Worksheet 2 – The World of the Brontës

A. Reread the information about the Brontës on pp. 157–158 of the graphic novel. Answer the questions.

1. What did the Brontë children do for fun? What does this tell you about the Brontës?

_____

_____

_____

2. Where did Emily spend most of her time? Why?

_____

_____

_____

3. Where did the Brontës live? Find out more about what this place was like using the library or the Internet. How might her surroundings have influenced Emily's writing?

_____

_____

_____

B. Read the statements about life in Victorian England. Decide if they are true or false. Circle your answers. Discuss your answers with the class.

1. Women could choose whatever profession they liked.	True	False
2. Men usually inherited property from their fathers; women had limited property rights.	True	False
3. Women often married for reasons of social status.	True	False
4. Female authors were respected as highly as male authors.	True	False
5. The ideal woman was bold, educated, independent, and expressed her feelings and opinions openly.	True	False
6. Many people died young.	True	False
7. Victorian doctors understood what caused diseases like tuberculosis.	True	False
8. One of the treatments for tuberculosis was getting fresh air or getting a change of air.	True	False
9. One of the causes of tuberculosis was poor sanitary conditions.	True	False
10. Victorian society was conservative. It valued tradition, good manners, and respect for the social hierarchy.	True	False

Name: _____

Before You Read

Worksheet 3 – Prepare to Discuss the Novel

A. Next to each statement, write R for Romantic novel, G for Gothic novel, or V for Victorian novel. (Some may have more than one answer!)

1. _____ There is a mysterious dark hero, who is not 100 percent good.
2. _____ The story takes place in an old house or castle.
3. _____ It includes a realistic description of life and events.
4. _____ The supernatural plays a big role, and there is often darkness and horror.
5. _____ It explores themes of social class and injustice.
6. _____ Nature plays a big role, and it is often tied to the emotions of the characters.
7. _____ The characters experience extreme states of emotion.
8. _____ There is a moral lesson and usually a happy ending.

B. Match the elements of a novel with their definitions. Write the correct letter on the line.

1. _____ climax   a. a person in a novel
2. _____ plot   b. problem or struggle between characters that creates tension and action
3. _____ setting   c. an important idea in a novel
4. _____ conflict   d. the most exciting part of a story, where the conflict is resolved and the main character or characters reach their goal
5. _____ theme   e. a location and time period where a novel or part of a novel takes place
6. _____ character   f. the action and events that happen in a story
7. _____ narrator   g. male protagonist, usually brave
8. _____ hero   h. a person who tells the story

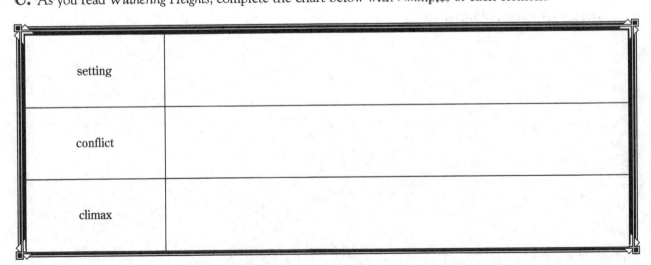

C. As you read *Wuthering Heights*, complete the chart below with examples of each element.

setting	
conflict	
climax	

Name: _____

A. Complete the story summary below using the words from the box. Use each word once. If you're not sure about the answer, guess!

lower class	isolated	mood	tenant	cruel	landlord
servant	unfriendly	wild	dignified	residents	brother

Wuthering Heights: A Preview

This story is about a(n) 1. _____ house in the English countryside called Wuthering Heights, and the people who live there, especially Catherine Earnshaw and Heathcliff, an orphan her father brings home from Liverpool to live with the family. Catherine and Heathcliff are both 2. _____ and free-spirited, and they form a very strong bond. Catherine's father loves Heathcliff, but her 3. _____ Hindley hates him and is 4. _____ to him. After Mr. Earnshaw dies, Hindley treats Heathcliff like a(n) 5. _____.

There is another house in the novel called Thrushcross Grange, where the Linton family lives. The Lintons are a(n) 6. _____, upper-class family. The young Lintons are named Edgar and Isabella. Young Heathcliff and Catherine see the young Lintons one night when they secretly walk out to Thrushcross Grange and peek into the window. One of the Lintons' dogs bites Catherine, and she ends up staying at the house for weeks. Heathcliff is not allowed into the house, because they think he is 7. _____.

But the story does not begin when Catherine and Heathcliff are young. It begins many years later, in 1801, when a man named Mr. Lockwood, a(n) 8. _____ at Thrushcross Grange, arrives at Wuthering Heights to meet his 9. _____, Mr. Heathcliff. Mr. Lockwood has a very odd experience there. The 10. _____ at the house is very dark, and Mr. Heathcliff is 11. _____ and quite mysterious. In order to piece together the history of the two houses and their 12. _____, Mr. Lockwood listens as the servant, Nelly Dean, who once worked at Wuthering Heights, tells the whole story.

B. Make predictions about the story below.

What do you think might happen between the following people when they grow up?

Heathcliff and Catherine: _____

_____

Heathcliff and Hindley: _____

_____

Catherine and Edgar Linton: _____

_____

Name: _____

Before You Read

Cut out the faces on p. 27 of this workbook. Then glue or tape them in the correct spaces below.

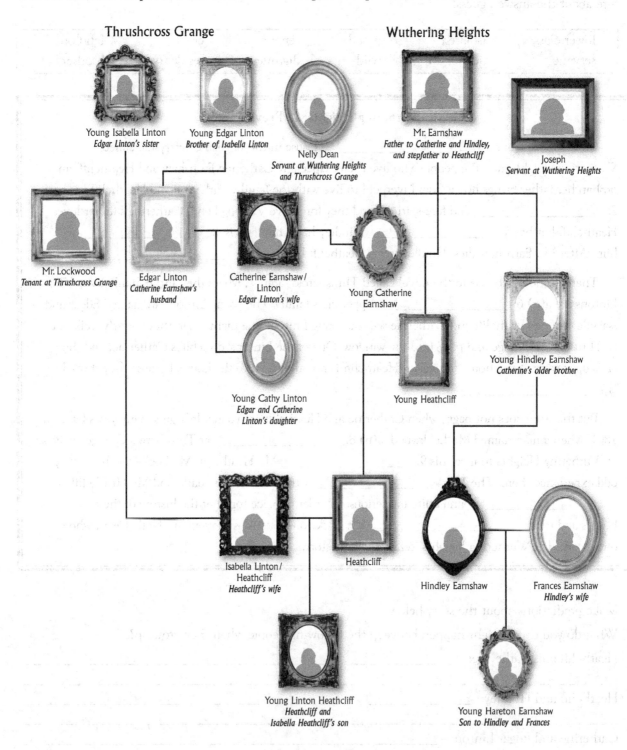

Thrushcross Grange

Wuthering Heights

Young Isabella Linton
Edgar Linton's sister

Young Edgar Linton
Brother of Isabella Linton

Nelly Dean
*Servant at Wuthering Heights
and Thrushcross Grange*

Mr. Earnshaw
*Father to Catherine and Hindley,
and stepfather to Heathcliff*

Joseph
Servant at Wuthering Heights

Mr. Lockwood
Tenant at Thrushcross Grange

Edgar Linton
*Catherine Earnshaw's
husband*

Catherine Earnshaw /
Linton
Edgar Linton's wife

Young Catherine
Earnshaw

Young Hindley Earnshaw
Catherine's older brother

Young Cathy Linton
*Edgar and Catherine
Linton's daughter*

Young Heathcliff

Isabella Linton /
Heathcliff
Heathcliff's wife

Heathcliff

Hindley Earnshaw

Frances Earnshaw
Hindley's wife

Young Linton Heathcliff
*Heathcliff and
Isabella Heathcliff's son*

Young Hareton Earnshaw
Son to Hindley and Frances

While You Read
Worksheet 6 – Chapters I–III

A. Choose the correct definition for each word in **bold**.

1. "I saw the name 'Hareton Earnshaw' and the year '1500' **carved** into the wall above the door." (p. 9)

   a. cut with a knife   **b.** painted   **c.** written

2. "Mr. Heathcliff dresses like a **gentleman**, but he seems to have a rough side." (p. 10)

   a. a servant   **b.** someone from the lower class   **c.** a man who is polite and educated

3. "They made me feel very **uncomfortable**." (p. 14)

   a. very angry   **b.** not relaxed   **c.** confident

4. "Mrs. Heathcliff is my **daughter-in-law**." (p. 15)

   a. son's wife   **b.** sister's daughter   **c.** adopted daughter

5. "I was **insulted**." (p. 16)

   a. offended   **b.** made to do something one doesn't want to do   **c.** comfortable

6. "What! Are we going to **murder** men on our own doorstep now?" (p. 16)

   a. welcome   **b.** kill   **c.** embarrass

CD 1
Tracks 1, 2

B. Listen to Chapters I and II as you follow along on pp. 7–16. Then read the statements below and decide if they are true or false. Circle your answers. If a statement is false, make it true and write it on the line.

1. Mr. Heathcliff is very friendly to Mr. Lockwood.   True   False

   _____

2. Mr. Lockwood returns to Wuthering Heights because the fireplace at Thrushcross Grange is not working properly.   True   False

   _____

3. Mr. Heathcliff's dogs attack Mr. Lockwood twice.   True   False

   _____

4. Mr. Heathcliff's son is dead.   True   False

   _____

5. Miss Catherine offers to walk Mr. Lockwood home.   True   False

   _____

6. Mr. Heathcliff invites Mr. Lockwood to stay the night because of the snow.   True   False

   _____

CD 1
Track 3

C. Listen to Chapter III as you follow along on pp. 17–23. Then answer the questions.

1. What does Mr. Lockwood find in the room?

   _____

2. What does Mr. Lockwood learn about young Catherine, Heathcliff, and Hindley?

   _____

   _____

3. Describe Mr. Lockwood's nightmare.

   _____

   _____

   _____

Name: _____

While You Read
Worksheet 7 – Chapters IV–VII

A. Match the words to the correct definitions.

1. _____ dignified
2. _____ furious
3. _____ grudge
4. _____ odd
5. _____ common
6. _____ rent
7. _____ complain
8. _____ escape

a. not refined; lower class
b. to get away from something
c. extremely angry
d. to say you are not satisfied with something
e. deserving respect
f. strange, unusual
g. unfriendly feelings for someone because of something that person did
h. an amount of money that a person pays to use a house or other quarters

CD 1
Tracks 4, 5

B. Listen as you read Chapters IV and V on pp. 23–27 of the graphic novel. Put the events of the story in order.

_____ Hindley goes away to college.
_____ Mr. Earnshaw goes on a trip to Liverpool.
_____ Mrs. Earnshaw dies.
_____ Catherine causes a lot of trouble.
_____ Nelly Dean begins to tell the story of Wuthering Heights.
_____ Mr. Earnshaw dies.
_____ Mr. Earnshaw brings back a young boy named Heathcliff.
_____ Catherine and Heathcliff become friends, and Hindley grows jealous.

CD 1
Tracks 6, 7

C. Listen to the audio and read Chapters VI and VII on pp. 28–37 in the graphic novel. Complete the paragraph with the missing information.

When Hindley came home for his father's funeral, he was _____. He began treating Heathcliff like a(n) _____. Heathcliff and Catherine would run away and stay out all day. One day, they went to _____ to look in the Lintons' window. The servants there thought they were _____ , so they released the dogs, and one of them bit _____. The Lintons insisted that she stay with them, but they would not let Heathcliff in because he was _____. Catherine stayed there for _____ weeks. She learned good _____ and how to act _____. When she came back to Wuthering Heights, she was very different. Heathcliff did not like the new Catherine. He was also jealous of _____, who was being raised as a refined gentleman. When Edgar Linton came to the house and _____ Heathcliff, Heathcliff attacked him. Hindley _____ him by locking him in his _____. Heathcliff began to plot his _____ against Hindley.

Name: _____

While You Read

Worksheet 8 – Chapters VIII–IX

A. Read Chapter VIII on pp. 38–43, and listen to the audio. Then fill in the chart below with the missing events that cause or are the result of other events.

Cause	Effect
	Frances dies.
Frances dies.	
	Catherine is all dressed up.
Heathcliff tells Catherine that he isn't going to work; he's going to stay with her.	
Edgar Linton arrives and Catherine asks Nelly to leave; Nelly doesn't leave.	
	Catherine slaps Edgar in the face.
	Catherine threatens to cry until she makes herself sick.
Catherine begins to cry.	

B. Match each vocabulary word to its opposite.

1. _____ disappearance   **a.** hell
2. _____ horrible   **b.** on purpose
3. _____ separated   **c.** appearance
4. _____ accidentally   **d.** divorce
5. _____ heaven   **e.** disgrace
6. _____ marriage   **f.** great, wonderful
7. _____ suffer   **g.** joined, put together
8. _____ honor   **h.** be happy, enjoy

C. Read the first part of Chapter IX, pp. 44–57. Then decide if the statements below are true or false. Correct the false statements.

1. Hindley comes home drunk, and Nelly hides Hareton from him.   True   False
   _____

2. Nelly uses a knife to protect herself from Hindley.   True   False
   _____

3. Hareton is happy to see his father.   True   False
   _____

4. Nelly accidentally drops Hareton over the railing upstairs.   True   False
   _____

5. Heathcliff arrives just in time and catches the baby.   True   False
   _____

6. Heathcliff is surprised that he saved Hareton's life.   True   False
   _____

While You Read

Worksheet 8 (continued)

CD 1
Track 9

D. Listen to the audio as you read the rest of Chapter IX, pp. 48–57. Catherine has just announced to Nelly her decision to marry Edgar Linton, but she is not sure that she is making the right decision. In the chart below, record Catherine's thoughts and feelings about Edgar and Heathcliff. Use her actual words from the graphic novel where possible.

	Edgar	Heathcliff
Catherine's reasons for marrying/not marrying him		
Catherine's true feelings about him		

E. Answer the following questions about Chapter IX.

1. Explain Catherine's dream. Why does she say, "I have no more reason to marry Edgar Linton than I have to be in heaven"?

_____

_____

_____

_____

2. What does Catherine do when she realizes that Heathcliff is missing? What is the result of her actions?

_____

_____

3. What happens when Mrs. Linton takes Catherine to Thrushcross Grange?

_____

4. How much time passes before Catherine marries Edgar? _____

_____

Name: _____

CD 1
Track 10

A. Listen to Chapter X and read along on pp. 58–65. Circle the correct words to complete the sentences.

1. At the beginning, it seems like Catherine and Edgar are **happy / miserable**.
2. One day, **Nelly / Catherine** sees Heathcliff in the garden.
3. Heathcliff looks **different / exactly the same**. He looks **dirty / gentlemanly** and **intelligent / wild**.
4. Catherine is **angry / happy** that Heathcliff has returned.
5. Heathcliff visits Thrushcross Grange **rarely / regularly**.
6. Isabella starts to **like / dislike** Heathcliff.
7. Isabella **pinches / scratches** Catherine when she grabs her and tells Heathcliff how she feels about him.
8. Edgar, Catherine, and Nelly know that Heathcliff wants to marry Isabella for her **money / beauty**.

CD 1
Track 11

B. Listen to the audio as you read Chapter XI on pp. 66–70.

1. Besides money, what reasons does Heathcliff have for pursuing Isabella?

_____

2. Why is Edgar angry at Heathcliff? What does he compare Heathcliff to?

_____

3. Why does Catherine turn against Edgar?

_____

_____

4. Explain the following quotes by Heathcliff:

   a. "Catherine, I want you to know that you were cruel to me. A few nice words will not make up for what you did."

   _____

   b. "I don't want revenge on you. A tyrant is cruel to people, but they don't turn against him – instead, they turn against those under them."

   _____

   c. "If I thought you really wanted me to marry Isabella, I'd probably kill myself!"

   _____

C. Replace the underlined word or phrase with the correct vocabulary word from Chapters X and XI.

coward	misery	heir to	weakling
approve of	sister-in-law	ignore	traitor

1. Isabella says that Catherine is enjoying her <u>unhappiness</u>. _____
2. Isabella is <u>the sister of Catherine's husband</u>. _____
3. Isabella is the <u>person who will inherit</u> Edgar's wealth. _____
4. Nelly calls Heathcliff a <u>person who has betrayed his friends</u> when she sees him kiss Isabella.

_____

5. Heathcliff says he will marry Isabella and <u>not pay any attention to</u> Catherine. _____
6. Catherine says that she thinks Edgar would <u>be happy about</u> Heathcliff's marriage to Isabella.

_____

7. Catherine calls Edgar a <u>person who is easily frightened</u> and a <u>person who is not strong</u> when he would not fight or apologize to Heathcliff. _____

_____

Name: _____

While You Read

Worksheet 10 – Chapters XII–XIV

CD 1
Track 12

A. Read Chapter XII on pp. 71–74. Read the statements below. Choose the word or phrase that means the same thing as the vocabulary word in **bold.**

1. Catherine is beginning to act **insane**.
   a. normal   **b.** crazy   **c.** unkind

2. Catherine thinks that the people around her are all **enemies**.
   a. people who hate each other   **b.** friends   **c.** ghosts

3. Catherine thought that no one could **resist liking her**.
   a. convince themselves to like her   **b.** explain why they like her   **c.** stop themselves from liking her

4. Catherine thinks she sees a face in the **chest** against the wall.
   a. the top part of the front of the body   **b.** a wooden chair   **c.** a piece of furniture that holds clothing

5. Really, she only sees her **reflection**.
   a. a portrait; painting of a person   **b.** your own image in a mirror   **c.** a dream or hallucination

6. Catherine **struggles** to get away from her husband.
   a. tries very hard   **b.** laughs   **c.** screams, cries

CD 1
Track 13

B. Read and listen to Chapter XIII on page 75. Answer the questions.

1. What do we learn about Catherine in this chapter? Give two reasons that Edgar wants her to get well.
   _____

2. What does Isabella's first letter reveal? What is Edgar's response?
   _____

3. How much time passes before Isabella writes her second letter? Whom does she write to?
   _____
   _____

4. What do we learn about Isabella and Heathcliff in Isabella's letter to Nelly? What does Isabella ask Nelly to do?
   _____
   _____

CD 1
Track 14

C. Listen to the audio and read Chapter XIV on pp. 76–79. Heathcliff is showing himself to be quite a bully. Fill in the chart with evidence from this chapter that Heathcliff is trying to control each of these characters.

Isabella	Nelly
Heathcliff thinks Nelly has brought a letter for Isabella, and he demands to see it.	
Edgar	**Catherine**

Name: _____

While You Read

Worksheet 11 – Chapters XV–XVII

CD 1
Track 15

A. Read Chapter XV on pp. 80–84. Decide if the statements below are true or false. Circle your answers. Correct the false statements.

1. Catherine is happy to see Heathcliff when he arrives.   True   False

_____

2. Catherine is no longer ill.   True   False

_____

3. Heathcliff tells Catherine that life will be torture for him if she continues to live with Edgar.   True   False

_____

4. Heathcliff and Catherine hold each other in their arms until Edgar arrives.   True   False

_____

5. Catherine asks Heathcliff to forgive her, and he does.   True   False

_____

6. Edgar is furious when he comes in to find Heathcliff with Catherine.   True   False

_____

7. Heathcliff goes back to Wuthering Heights.   True   False

_____

CD 1
Track 16

B. Read Chapter XVI on pp. 85–88. Circle the correct word or phrase to complete each statement.

1. Catherine gives birth to a baby **girl / boy**.
2. Nelly feels **sorry for / angry at** Heathcliff.
3. Heathcliff hopes that Catherine wakes up **in heaven / tortured**.
4. Heathcliff calls Catherine a **liar / coward**.
5. Heathcliff asks Catherine to **kill / haunt** him.
6. **Edgar / Nelly** stays by Catherine's coffin day and night.
7. Heathcliff comes in the **window / back door** to visit Catherine's body.
8. He puts a **photo / lock of his hair** in Catherine's locket.

CD 1
Track 17

C. Read Chapter XVII on pp. 89–96. Complete the paragraph with the correct vocabulary words.

involved	gambling	grieve	neighborhood
property	dreary	inherit	cruelty

Edgar did not 1. _____ for his wife Catherine for very long or ask for her to haunt him. Instead, he gave his attention to his daughter, Cathy. Nelly helped him. One day, when Nelly was sitting with Cathy, Isabella arrived at Thrushcross Grange. She had escaped from her 2._____ life at Wuthering Heights and the 3. _____ of her husband, Heathcliff. She told Nelly the story of a terrible fight that happened between Hindley and Heathcliff. Afterward, Isabella left the 4. _____ of Thrushcross Grange and moved to London. There, she gave birth to a son, whom she named Linton. She died when he was twelve. In the meantime, Nelly learned that Hindley Earnshaw had also died, from drinking too much. He had sold all of his 5. _____ to Heathcliff to pay off his 6. _____ debts. So Hindley's son Hareton would not 7. _____ anything. Nelly wondered if Heathcliff was 8. _____ in Hindley's death.

While You Read

Worksheet 12 – Chapters XVIII–XXI

A. Explain the meaning of each underlined vocabulary word.

1. No one <u>celebrates</u> Cathy's birthday because it was also the day her mother died.

_____

2. Edgar never <u>scolds</u> Cathy, even when she behaves badly.

_____

3. One day, Cathy rides her <u>pony</u> to Wuthering Heights.

_____

4. Cathy's cousin Linton is very sickly, <u>pale</u>, and <u>delicate</u>.

_____

5. Edgar and Heathcliff had a <u>disagreement</u> many years ago, so Edgar does not want Cathy to visit Wuthering Heights.

_____

6. Nelly hopes that Heathcliff will be <u>proud</u> of his son, Linton, and treat him well.

_____

7. Heathcliff is very <u>moody</u>.

_____

CD 2
Tracks 2,3,4

B. Read Chapters XVIII, XIX, and XX on pp. 97–103. Listen to the audio. Then put the events of the story in the correct order.

_____ Joseph arrives to take Linton to Wuthering Heights, but Edgar sends him away.
_____ Cathy meets her cousin Linton.
_____ Cathy meets her cousin Hareton at Wuthering Heights.
_____ Cathy turns thirteen.
_____ Heathcliff promises to treat Linton kindly.
_____ Nelly takes Linton to Wuthering Heights.
_____ Isabella dies.
_____ Cathy rides off alone on her pony.

CD 2
Track 5

C. Read Chapter XXI on pp. 104–109 and listen to the audio. Answer the questions.

1. What does Cathy do on her sixteenth birthday?

_____

2. What does Heathcliff tell Nelly about his plans for Cathy?

_____

3. How does Cathy feel about her cousin Hareton? How does she treat him?

_____

4. How does Cathy feel about her cousin Linton? What happens between them?

_____

5. How does Edgar react when he learns that Cathy visited Wuthering Heights?

_____

6. How does Nelly react when she finds letters from Linton in Cathy's room?

_____

Name: _____

CD 2
Tracks 6, 7

A. Listen to the audio as you read Chapters XXII and XXIII on pp. 110–114. Then complete the summary below with the missing information.

    One day, Cathy climbs over the _____ and is locked out. Heathcliff stops by and sees her. He tells her that Linton is _____ because she stopped writing to him, and that she must go and see him. Nelly tells her not to _____, but Cathy is very worried about Linton. She and Nelly go the next day.

    Linton is _____ to see Catherine, but he is _____ that she hasn't visited. He hopes that Cathy doesn't _____ him. She says that she _____ him more than anyone after her father and Nelly, but that she doesn't love Heathcliff because he is _____. Linton doesn't believe Cathy when she tells him that his mother _____. He tells Cathy that her mother hated _____ and loved _____. Cathy gets angry at him and _____. He starts coughing. She feels very bad. Linton tells Cathy that she _____ it to him to come back and visit, because she _____ him.

    When they leave, Cathy asks Nelly whether or not she likes Linton. Nelly thinks he is _____. Nelly tells Cathy that she can't have any more contact with Linton.

B. Explain the meaning of each of these sentences containing a vocabulary word in **bold**. Use details from the novel in your explanation.

1. Cathy does not **obey** Nelly's orders.

_____

2. Nelly **betrays** Cathy to Edgar.

_____

3. Edgar **forbids** Cathy to return to Wuthering Heights.

_____

4. But Edgar starts to change his mind. He does not want to **abandon** Cathy when he dies.

_____

5. He does not want Cathy to be with a man who is **unworthy**.

_____

6. He doesn't care if Heathcliff **robs** him of everything, so long as Cathy is taken care of.

_____

7. Nelly believes that Cathy will do the right thing and be **rewarded**.

_____

CD 2
Track 10

C. Read and listen to Chapter XXVI on pp. 118–119. Answer the questions.

1. What does Linton ask for in his letter to Edgar? Why?

_____

2. How does Linton look when Cathy meets him?

_____

3. How does Linton behave during their meeting?

_____

4. What is Edgar's reaction to their meeting?

_____

Name: _____

While You Read
Worksheet 14 – Chapters XXVII–XXIX

A. Match the vocabulary words to their definitions.

1. _____ remind
2. _____ prisoner
3. _____ remain
4. _____ belongings
5. _____ spirit

a. stay in a particular place or condition
b. things that a person owns
c. make a person think of someone or something
d. ghost; the soul or essence of a person who has died
e. a person who is locked up and not allowed to leave, usually in punishment for a crime

CD 2
Track 11

B. Read Chapter XXVII on pp. 120–128 and listen to the audio. Then list four cruel things that Heathcliff does in this chapter.

Heathcliff's cruelty
1.
2.
3.
4.

CD 2
Track 12

C. Read Chapter XXVIII on pp. 129–132 and listen to the audio. Then decide if the statements below are true or false. Circle your answer.

1. Zillah knew that Nelly was a prisoner at Heathcliff's house. — True False
2. When Nelly finds Linton downstairs, he is sad and very sorry about his father's actions. — True False
3. Linton gives Nelly the key to Cathy's room. — True False
4. Nelly sends servants to Wuthering Heights to get Cathy and to bring their lawyer. — True False
5. Edgar wants to write a will to prevent Heathcliff from getting his property after he dies. — True False
6. The servants bring Cathy back. — True False
7. Cathy tells Edgar the truth about what happened to her at Wuthering Heights. — True False
8. The lawyer arrives just in time, before Edgar dies. — True False

CD 2
Track 13

D. Read Chapter XXIX on pp. 133–135 and listen to the audio. Answer the questions.

1. When does Heathcliff arrive to take possession of Thrushcross Grange and to take Cathy back to Wuthering Heights?

_____

2. Why does Heathcliff want Cathy and Linton to stay at Thrushcross Grange, even though he hates them?

_____

3. Why does Cathy feel sorry for Heathcliff?

_____

4. What story does Heathcliff tell about his actions after Catherine's death?

_____

5. When Cathy tells Nelly to visit her often, what is Heathcliff's reaction?

_____

Name: _____

While You Read

Worksheet 15 – Chapters XXX–XXXIV

CD 2
Tracks 14, 15

A. Listen to the audio as you read Chapters XXX and XXXI on pp. 136–137. Then decide if the statements are true or false. Circle your answers.

1. Cathy goes straight to Linton's room when she gets to Wuthering Heights, and she finds him sick.
       True   False
2. Heathcliff sends for a doctor.
       True   False
3. Cathy helps a nurse take care of Linton.
       True   False
4. After Linton dies, Cathy feels better that he is safe, and she is free.
       True   False
5. Linton leaves everything to Heathcliff in his will, so Cathy has nothing.
       True   False
6. Lockwood decides to leave Thrushcross Grange.
       True   False
7. Lockwood has a pleasant dinner at Wuthering Heights.
       True   False

CD 2
Track 16

B. Listen to the audio as you read Chapter XXXII on pp. 138–141. Then answer the questions.

1. Why does Mr. Lockwood come back to Thrushcross Grange?

_____

2. What news does he learn about Heathcliff?

_____

3. What news does he learn about Hareton and Cathy?

_____

CD 2
Tracks 17, 18

C. Listen to the audio and read Chapters XXXIII and XXXIV on pp. 142–150. Complete the summary with the correct vocabulary words.

witch	selfish	gravestones	grip	mutters	complain
releases	beggar	unbearable	hideous	conscience	soaking wet

> Joseph and Heathcliff become furious over some bushes that Hareton cleared from the garden when Cathy asked him to. Cathy tells Heathcliff he shouldn't _____ about a small bit of garden when he has stolen all her land and all of Hareton's land. Heathcliff becomes angry and calls Cathy a _____ for turning Hareton against him. He grabs her and threatens to hit her, but then he _____ his _____. He tells her that he will throw Hareton out and make him a _____ if he listens to her again. But later he tells Nelly that he doesn't enjoy getting revenge on his enemies' children anymore. He feels a change coming. Life is _____ for him now. He wants to die and be with Catherine again. Nelly thinks that he has a guilty _____.
>
> Heathcliff begins to act strangely and _____ to himself. Nelly suggests that he talk to someone from the church because he has led a _____ and terrible life. Heathcliff says that he will be entering his own heaven. The next evening, it rains heavily all night. Nelly notices that Heathcliff's window is open. She finds him lying on his bed _____ and dead. He has a _____ smile on his face. Heathcliff is buried next to Catherine.
>
> Nelly tells Lockwood that Hareton and Cathy are to be married. Lockwood leaves Thrushcross Grange and visits the _____ of Edgar, Catherine, and Heathcliff before he goes.

After You Read
Worksheet 16 – Matching Quotes

A. Cut out all the cards and match each quote to the character that said it.

"I had a tough life, but I got through it. It was all for you."	**Nelly Dean**
"Wouldn't you feel guilty if I fell into a pit and died?"	**Edgar Linton**
"Stay calm. Don't let the household see you greeting a servant like a brother."	**Isabella Linton/ Heathcliff**
"By making others miserable, you make yourself miserable. I feel sorry for you. Nobody will cry for you when you die!"	**Hindley Earnshaw**
"She has gone to heaven, I hope. We can all join her, if we reject evil and do good in our lives."	**Heathcliff**
"I live only for him. He is always on my mind. I can't be separated from him. I won't do it."	**Linton Heathcliff**

Name: _____

"Shame on you for misbehaving. Sit down and read your prayer books."	**Catherine Earnshaw/ Linton**
"Look at this! A gift for everyone!"	**Zillah**
"What! Are we going to murder men on our own doorstep now? Look at the poor thing – he's almost choking."	**Joseph**
"I ran all the way from Wuthering Heights. I ran away. Please help me get to the village."	**Mr. Earnshaw**
"Get out of here, Heathcliff! Did you brush your hair for the first time?"	**Cathy Linton**
"Mother never told me I had a father. Where does he live?"	**Lockwood**

Name: _____

After You Read
Worksheet 17 – Exploring Themes

A. Working in pairs or small groups, use the following table to explore some themes in *Wuthering Heights: The Graphic Novel*. Find a scene in the novel where the theme is present, and give evidence from the novel (a quotation or a description of an event). Explain in what way the quotation or event that you have chosen illustrates the theme. One row has been left blank so that you can add another theme that you identify.

Themes	Chapter/Page	Quotation or Event and Explanation
Love and passion		
Social class (its importance and its instability)		
Revenge/punishment		
Wild nature vs. civilized culture		

Name: _____

Worksheet 17 (continued)—Exploring Themes

B. Look at the elements of a Gothic novel in the first column of the chart. In the second column, indicate whether each element can be found in *Wuthering Heights: The Graphic Novel*. In the third column, give an example from the story.

Element	Yes/No	Example
Set in a castle	No	Set in an old house
Supernatural elements		
Darkness, shadow		
Sense of fear or mystery		
Death, deterioration, decay		
An ancient prophecy or curse		
Extreme states of emotion		
Women who are trapped or threatened by a powerful man		
Forbidden passions vs. social conventions		
A flawed hero, a villain, or a hero/villain		

After You Read

Worksheet 18 – Characters' Diary Entries

A. Choose one of the characters below. Then choose one of the parts of the novel listed. Imagine that you are the character. Write your thoughts and feelings at that stage of the novel in a diary entry.

Edgar
_____

1. While Catherine is first staying at his house (Chapters VI and VII)
_____

2. After Heathcliff first returns to Thrushcross Grange (Chapter X)
_____

3. Right after Isabella runs away with Heathcliff (Chapter XII)
_____

Heathcliff
_____

1. Soon after Mr. Earnshaw brings Heathcliff to Wuthering Heights (Chapter IV)
_____

2. The night of Catherine's death (Chapter XVI)
_____

3. Right after Linton's death, when Cathy and Hareton start to become friends (Chapter XXXIII)
_____

Catherine
_____

1. After her father dies and Hindley becomes the man of the house (Chapter VI)
_____

2. After Heathcliff leaves Wuthering Heights (Chapter IX)
_____

3. After Heathcliff first returns to Thrushcross Grange (Chapter X)
_____

Cathy
_____

1. The day she first visits Wuthering Heights (Chapter XVIII)
_____

2. While she is imprisoned at Wuthering Heights by Heathcliff (Chapters XXVII and XXVIII)
_____

3. After Heathcliff's death (Chapter XXXIV)
_____

B. Write your diary entry in the spaces below.

_____
_____
_____
_____
_____
_____
_____

Name: _____

A. Read the article.

The Yorkshire Country Telegraph
LATE EDITION

NOVEMBER 25, 1801

London visitor attacked by landlord's dogs, visited by ghost

Mr. Lockwood, a tenant at the former Linton estate, Thrushcross Grange, met with a strange and violent incident when he visited his landlord, Mr. Heathcliff, at Wuthering Heights. Lockwood claims that he was "insulted" by the strange family. "It was late at night. No one would help me get home, and they refused to let me stay the night," claims Lockwood. "When I tried to borrow a lantern, they set the dogs on me!"

Lockwood was not seriously injured, but the attack was psychologically traumatizing. Although he was later allowed to stay the night, there was more excitement in store for him. Lockwood claims that he was visited by a ghost in his room. He says that it was the ghost of Catherine Earnshaw Linton, who lived at Wuthering Heights as a child. Was it a nightmare, or is Wuthering Heights haunted?

B. Choose an event in the graphic novel. Write a newspaper article about it.

_____
_____
_____
_____
_____
_____
_____
_____
_____
_____
_____

Name: _____

In this worksheet, your class will put Heathcliff from *Wuthering Heights* on trial for theft, cruelty, and abuse. To conduct a trial, you will need people to fill several different roles. Decide who will fill each of the following roles in your classroom courtroom:

- The judge: _____
- The jury: _____
- The accused: _____

- The prosecution: _____
- The defense: _____
- Witnesses: _____

Whatever your role is, you will need to think about the case. In the space below, make notes. If you are a lawyer, a witness, or the accused, plan what you will say. What are your arguments? What is your evidence? How will you persuade the judge and the jury to sympathize with you and decide in your favor? Remember, the goal of the prosecution is to show that Heathcliff is guilty and does not deserve sympathy. The goal of the defense is to show that Heathcliff is worthy of sympathy, and that the circumstances of his life led him to his actions, many of which were legal and justifiable.

If you are a judge or part of the jury: Make notes during the case about the arguments on each side. Try to be fair and impartial. You're ready to start the trial!

_____
_____
_____
_____
_____
_____
_____
_____
_____
_____
_____
_____
_____
_____

Name: _____

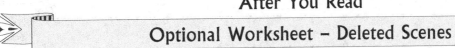

Scenario 1	**Parts: 2+**	Mr. Earnshaw is in Liverpool on his business trip. He finds Heathcliff and decides to take him to Wuthering Heights.
Scenario 2	**Parts: 2**	Catherine's spirit visits Heathcliff after her death. This could be immediately after her death, or it could be later, closer to Heathcliff's death.
Scenario 3	**2+**	Heathcliff has left Wuthering Heights. This scene shows where he has gone and what he does to earn his wealth.
Scenario 4	**2**	It's shortly after Edgar and Heathcliff argued and Edgar sent Heathcliff away. Heathcliff is meeting with Isabella. They plan to run away and get married.
Scenario 5	**2**	Edgar talks to Isabella about his plans to marry Catherine. This could be before or after his visit to Wuthering Heights on the night that Heathcliff runs away.
Scenario 6	**Parts: 2 or 3**	Heathcliff is at home with Linton. Does Heathcliff bully Linton into the idea of trapping and marrying Cathy, or is Linton willing and happy to go along with it? You decide! (You may add a third character, Hareton. We don't see much of Hareton in this part of story in the graphic novel—Is he in on the plot, too? Does he approve, or does he protest?)

Appendix

The Brontës' Works

Emily Brontë

1847	*Wuthering Heights*

Charlotte Brontë

1847	*Jane Eyre*
1849	*Shirley—A Tale*
1853	*Villette*
1854	*Emma* (an unfinished novel)
1847	*The Professor* (published after she died)

Anne Brontë

1847	*Agnes Grey*
1848	*The Tenant of Wildfell Hall*

Brontë Sisters

1846	*Poems* by Currer, Ellis, and Acton Bell (pseudonyms for Charlotte, Emily, and Anne)

Extra Resources

Wuthering Heights:

http://www.literature.org/authors/bronte-emily/wuthering-heights/
http://www.shmoop.com/wuthering-heights/
http://www.sparknotes.com/lit/wuthering/

Emily Brontë:

http://www.bronte.info/
http://www.literaryhistory.com/19thC/BRONTEE.htm
www.online-literature.com/bronte/
http://academic.brooklyn.cuny.edu/english/melani/novel_19c/wuthering/index.html

Victorian Literature and Culture:

http://victorianweb.org/

Name: _____

Cut out the faces. Glue or tape them in the correct places on Worksheet 5.